Published by
Scope Books Ltd.,
62 Murray Road,
Horndean
Hants PO8 9JL

2nd Edition 1988

By Dr. W.G. Hill J.D.
Investigator and Consultant

For questions and further information contact the author by mail:
SOS WESTANCO, P.O. BOX HM 1721, Hamilton, Bermuda HMGX

British Library Cataloguing in Publication Data

Hill, William G.
The Monaco report : the advantages of
Monaco as a tax haven.—2nd ed.
1. Tax havens
I. Title
336.2'06 K4464.5

ISBN 0-906619-16-5

Phototypeset by Barbara James Typesetting, Hayling Island, Hampshire
Printed by Richard Clay, Chichester, Sussex

CONTENTS

WHAT IS A TAX HAVEN?

The German word for it is *Steueroase* — tax oasis: in French it's *un paradis fiscal* — a money paradise. In English, the word "haven" derives from harbor, "safe harbor". Just as every harbor has special features, every tax haven is different. Finding the one suitable for you involves knowing and comparing the features of each, thus finding the proper haven for your needs.

In the world today there are three types of tax havens:

Type 1. A place having the legal facilities making it suitable for headquartering a multi-national business, managing substantial personal or holding trusts/foundations/corporations. Within the United States, for instance, the State of Delaware has made its state laws and taxes very favorable to large corporations. In Europe, Luxembourg, Liechtenstein and the Channel Islands fill the same function. For shipping magnates, the best place to be legally headquartered is Liberia or Panama. A favorite haven of this type will seldom be a place where individuals would want to live. Obviously there is nothing illegal about taking advantage of a favorable domicile.

Type 2. A place that is mixed: desirable both for living and for the incorporation or headquartering of administrative functions: Bermuda, Hong Kong and the Channel Islands fall into this category.

Type 3. A place that is safe and pleasant for civilized individuals to live in. They are most rare! There are a number of oddball coral reefs and forgotten third world backwaters like Belize, Paraguay or Palau that individuals use. And there is something to be said for being a resident of a tax haven nobody has ever heard of — particularly if you are not really going to live there much. For sheer boredom you can't beat the many Pacific Trust Territories of the United States. But for boredom plus the worst weather in the world the French island of St. Pierre and Miquelon gets the grand prize. In this writer's opinion, the list of truly liveable tax havens for sophisticated, pleasure loving individuals is limited to only one place: Monaco. Monaco is the subject of this Report. To appreciate Monaco it is necessary to consider the alternatives.

RATING THE TAX HAVENS

Preparing a list and saying "This one is best; second best; third best" and so on does not work very well for tax havens. The reason is that they all have different characteristics. Also they may offer only certain types of people (or companies) preference. These preferences may be because of a specific government plan, or because things just happened to work out that way because of history. Does it matter? Yes it does! A program instituted by a political party that has just taken control by a narrow electoral victory is less likely to be around in five or ten years than a situation that has already been in place for 2,000 years. Andorra, Bermuda, Cayman, Monaco, Sark and Pitcairn *have never had income taxes.* They did not abolish tax just to attract wealthy retirees. It is possible to make a judgment on this factor. I call it "Stability". Stability may not be important to you. If, for instance one liked the Monaco life style but kept assets elsewhere (as we advise in this Report) it wouldn't matter if all of a sudden Monaco instituted a 10% annual wealth tax and a 50% income tax. Assuming they didn't close the borders (like Communist states do) you could simply abandon your rented apartment, forget about your small checking account, and take a powder. In a few years, of course, Monaco would be a shadow of its former grandeur, as its wealthy population scattered all over the world. This is exactly what happened in historic tax havens like Algiers, Casablanca, Danzig, — or if you want to go back to one of the original tax havens, to the Greek island of Delos, the Monaco of the Roman Empire.

The questions you must answer when determining which tax havens you will use (if any) are these:

Do I have enough taxable income to make the whole exercise worthwhile? Though there is no "rule", my rule of thumb would be that if you pay taxes and have enough income to live without working at a job, tax havens are worth a look at. Or, if you have an income that could be earned without living in the high tax jurisdiction where you live now, you might consider using a tax haven.

Do I pay enough taxes, or am I sufficiently annoyed with the record-keeping requirements and possible penalties that I should move myself or my business elsewhere? This is a personal decision that only you can make.

Is there a substantial risk that war, revolution, political changes, etc, would make my life miserable enough so that I should consider establishing a safe haven for future use? In this case, obtaining a second passport and merely renting a modest studio in Monaco to establish an escape route would be well advised; just a modest dose of preparedness. The author's opinion is that anyone who can afford a second passport and a second residence outside of the home country should have one.

Am I inflexible enough so that I want to be only where everyone understands my language; and local customs, laws and life in general are pretty much the same as "at home"? This narrows the choice considerably, but for English speakers whose language is spoken in virtually all tax havens as a first or second language, the outlook is bright. You can live amongst people very much like those you left behind. In Monaco there are expatriate sub-groups of all nationalities.

Do I want glamour, conspicuous consumption, opera, live theatre, discos, high fashion, topless beaches, gambling casinos, celebrities, 5 Star hotels and restaurants, film and jazz festivals, Formula One auto races, high society parties, an opportunity to dress-up in white tie and tails a few times a year, and a tuxedo every night if desired? Then Monaco is the only tax haven that fills the bill. If you want a laid back existence with skiing, hunting, fishing — try Andorra, Panama, Costa Rica. Want to be a hermit? The British protectorate Pitcairn's your place, with St. Pierre and Miquelon (French) as an alternative if you want to be a very cold hermit.

A few countries that are not considered tax havens at all may be tax havens for you because of special provisions to attract certain types of people or industry. Take New Zealand for instance. In general New Zealand has perhaps the world's highest tax burden. But to attract entrepreneurs or investors who will create jobs, promote exports, or develop tourist destinations, New Zealand will grant what amounts to a lifetime tax holiday. Highly taxed Israel will do the same thing! Incredibly — so will Poland!

This is not the place for discussing all these special deals, but a very active industrialist or mover and shaker might find greener pastures elsewhere than Monaco. Monaco in general is for individuals who have already made their money and want now to let others run the store while they practise the art of living. Monaco is for people who want to spend time on the Riviera. If pure tax avoidance is the motive, there are cheaper ways to do it than renting an apartment in Monaco, although one can live cheaply there with some effort. As of 1987, the rock-bottom cheapest rent in Monaco was about $75 per month. This seven hundred French francs in monthly rent gets you a one-maid's room on the top floor of an older seven storey walk-up. The toilet we saw was a primitive shared arrangement, down the hall. A room such as this may also be purchased for around F*f*200,000.

Unfortunately, the Monaco police will not recognize a facility without a proper kitchen and bath for legal residence purposes. The most grotty legally recognized "residence" would be found in the port area. There your one room would hold a single bed and a chair, but you'd have a tiny bathroom and kitchen. The view? Forget it! But for those readers interested in minimum compliance, such an apartment recently sold for $37,000, in an otherwise decent elevator building. The owner then asked $375 per month rent — which would have given him a nice tax free return had anyone paid it. But it ultimately rented for $275 to an individual with a very nice home a few miles away, who wanted a respectable Monaco address. A pleasant studio with a decent view, marble floors and good appliances would rent for £300 or US $450. (Author's note: The exchange rate of F*f*9 per US $1 in effect in early '86 is alas, no longer. As of early 1988, the prices expressed here in dollars must be raised by 50%. As this book goes to print a dollar buys just over 5 French francs).

Monaco would be the logical first choice for an individual desiring urban pleasures and who likes the goodies that the French and Italians are famous for. As noted above, although Monaco has the reputation of being terribly expensive, a little bargain hunting can turn up the occasional dump. As to food, one can spend $15 on an elaborate buffet breakfast at the Monte Carlo Beach Hotel — or do as I did this morning: walk two blocks uphill to the public market place in Beausoleil, and select from several hundred cheeses, paté, olives, pickles, cold cuts and fresh fruits. For about two dollars, I put together a little spread accompanied with a delicious cappuccino coffee and a baguette of French bread. The coffee bar in the market will (for the price of a drink) supply a sharp knife and a table where you can watch the haggling, joking and market activities of a typical French village. You are one city block and a hundred light years away from Monaco. In 1987 I made a bet that I could live for a month in Monaco — hotel, food, the works for under $15 per day. I won the bet! I mention this only to show that you can find what you need, at a price you want to spend, even in Monaco!

Reading this Report should eliminate most surprises, but there is no substitute for a personal visit. Any visit will be greatly enhanced by personal contacts. Looking at rentals and properties for sale is a quick way to meet a wide variety of people and get answers to most of your questions.

If you have access to a business or commercial library near your present home there are several journals and other publications (primarily for accountants and lawyers) that are worth looking at: *Tax Haven and Shelter Report*, *International Tax Report* and *Tax Planning International*. Reference books include: *Tax Havens* by Walter and D.B. Diamond; *Butterworth's Tax Havens Encyclopaedia* edited by Barry Spitz; *Foreign Tax Planning* and other books by USA attorney Marshall Langer; *Tax Havens* by Milton Grundy; *Using Tax Havens Successfully* by Edouard Chambost and Thomas Crawley. A few years back, there were many good articles and books coming out of the USA, but we understand that the IRS now has a policy of putting authors of tax avoidance books in jail. As a result, the more amusing American writers (Irwin Schiff: *How Anyone Can Avoid Taxes*, are too busy breaking rocks or whatever prisoners do, to tweak the tail of the tax collectors any more. If you discover anything interesting on the subject of tax havens send me a copy, the author will try to reciprocate with some new article, book or other goody.

Incidentally, it should be noted that most tax agencies have considerable powers to interfere with your departure or transfer of assets to foreign countries — even where there are NO exchange controls. Obviously your intentions should not be broadcast. This Report for instance, should not be prominently displayed on your desk at work — or in your home for that matter, unless your spouse fully shares your objectives and ideas about personal freedom.

PERMANENT TOURISTS AND PERPETUAL TRAVELERS

For those who can live comfortably with the idea of having "no fixed and regular place of abode", the whole world is a giant tax haven. If one does not stay more than six months in most countries, one is considered a tourist. A perpetual tourist never is taxed. Thousands of retired people are permanent tourists in Mexico and Italy (to name just two examples). The local authorities know them as being from somewhere else — usually the country of their passport. But they seldom, if ever, become legally registered "permanent residents". The country where they have their fiscal (official) address is chosen because it doesn't want to extract any tax, military service or other unwanted obligations. If they wish to be in technical compliance with the local law, they can take a short drive or walk across the nearest border twice a year. Others, wanting to explore the world will follow the sun anyway, tending to move with the seasons. They drive tax-free cars, drink tax-free booze and sample the best things the world has to offer, seldom staying more than six months in any one home. Obviously, to be this kind of tax traveler requires a business or income that is not tied to any one particular physical location. An investment portfolio managed from Zurich, London, Tokyo or New York can support the "ideal lifestyle". A permanent mailing address (preferably in a tax haven) is needed by a footloose individual. This permanent travel option, with a few twists, is explored in our special report on Sark, Channel Islands. But for now, let's look at the runner-up tax havens to highly liveable Monaco, and see what they have to offer. Remember, you don't have to purchase a home or commit yourself to spending a lifetime there.

BERMUDA: Pink coral sand beaches. First class hotels and restaurants. It's great for a month, but one quickly gets "rock fever" and a desire to get on the next plane out of this tiny island. But that is my personal view. Many wealthy individuals have chosen to make their homes on Bermuda or similar dots on your map. The multi-millionaire founder manager of the John Templeton Fund — who could certainly afford to live anywhere in the world — has chosen a similar Caribbean tax haven, the Bahamas. The cost of a home, food, gasoline, household help in Bermuda is about double that of Monaco. Living expenses? Say $70,000 per year for a couple. Visit Bermuda. Maybe you'd like it.

ANDORRA: A favorite for retired English of moderate circumstances. The cost of everything is less than half that of Monaco. But it is as remote as Bermuda; a land-locked Catalonian principality in the French-Spanish Pyrenees, it's primarily a ski resort. The only nearby city is Barcelona. Barcelona can be a seven hour drive in the winter. Two could live well here on $14,000 per annum. Booze, skiing, gasoline, gadgets are about as cheap here as anywhere in the world. The climate is like Aspen, Colorado or Saint Moritz, Switzerland.

CAMPIONE: A favorite of the Germans. An apartment would be about the same cost as in Monaco, and food costs are about the same. Campione, though inside of the Italian speaking part of Switzerland, actually has a sand beach with swaying palm trees. Add a few hula dancers and you'd think you were in Hawaii. It also has a famous casino, and is much like Monaco was in 1949; undiscovered and sleepy! A short (under twenty minutes) drive or ferry boat ride from the major

Swiss cities of Lugano, Locarno and Chiasso. It is also close to Como and the Milan International Airport. The climate is not as warm as Monaco but it seldom freezes in winter. It's not much of an international tourist destination (although Italians crowd the casino). The total population is only about 3,000 — less than 10% of Monaco's population. There are no hotels! In area it is about the same size as Monaco: half a square mile. It has a major advantage over Monaco: no exchange controls and the convenience of Switzerland's third largest banking city (Lugano) just across the lake — a few pennies and ten minutes away by ferry. The postal system and telephones are run by the efficient Swiss. Campione residents get a Swiss driver's license, Swiss car plates, and an open border with Switzerland. It lacks the glitter, glamour and high-society of Monaco. One of these days I'll write a report on Campione. I've visited the place several dozen times and find it quaint and charming. If you want to be on the list to receive a pre-publication copy, drop me a line. Living costs for two: $35,000 per annum or about Swiss francs 60,000 and up. Same as Monaco. To become a resident you buy or rent an apartment and register with the police. Just like Monaco.

The three personal tax havens named are all prosperous, and the local population would rather fight (or move) than pay taxes. They do not resent rich foreigners who have settled amongst them. Other tax havens were not mentioned here because of political instability, poverty, extreme remoteness. But in case you want to check out a few obscure locales in the Encyclopaedia Britannica, here are some of the no-tax or low tax jurisdictions where a prosperous individual could immigrate if so inclined: Albania, St. Helena, Liberia, Pitcairn, Turks and Caicos, Cayman, Costa Rica, Belize, Channel Islands, Nauru, Paraguay, Svalbard, Hong Kong, Macau, United Arab Emirates, Falkland Islands.

On the above list, I might take a serious second look at Costa Rica and Hong Kong — but only because of the fact that they are also considered paradises for middle aged gents who enjoy young girls. Does anyone out there want a Special Report on THAT subject? We could call it "Sex Havens for Tax Fiends"? As a matter of fact, I'm personally researching this topic as you read this book. Should you want a look at my experience in Phucket, Thailand; drop me a note.

MONTE CARLO, MONACO

The city is called Monte Carlo. The country or "Principality", is Monaco. Inside Monaco, "Monte

Carlo'' is used to describe the neighborhood around the Casino. Although there are three casinos now, ''The'' Casino is the old one in the Belle Epoch structure that is a miniature version of the Paris Opera House. The new ones are at Loew's and The Sporting Club.

Unlike most other tax havens, Monaco is not physically isolated. It is at the centre of bright lights and action: the legendary French Riviera! The incredibly magnificent turn-of-the-century Hotel du Paris, and the Hotel Hermitage look clean, and in perfect state — as if they were built yesterday. Yet they have an elegance and class found nowhere else. The same can be said of the chic patrons! Across the street at Loew's Hotel and Casino, high-rollers fresh from Las Vegas and Atlantic City will gamble American style. Floor shows are flown in from Vegas or Paris. The doormen and headwaiters are haughty, turning away those without jackets and ties at the Opera House (''The'' Casino). If you appear to be a ''somebody'', they'll bend the rules for you. Like Beverly Hills, there's lots of flash. A good tip buys instant obsequience. The parking lots are crowded with Rolls Royces, Ferraris, antique Deusenbergs, and other exotic vehicles. They bear equally exotic license plates: Kuwait, Andorra, Liechtenstein, Gibraltar. When you see ''Monte Carlo 1'', the Prince or his rock-star daughter Princess Stephanie is in attendance!

BENEATH THE GLITTER

There are a lot of celebrities, aristocrats, filthy rich folks, phoneys and hangers-on milling about. But who are the average Monte Carlo residents? The vast majority do not drive a Rolls or come very often to play thousand dollar chips at the Casino. They are in fact upper middle-class retired individuals who have moved to Monaco for its ambience, pleasant Mediterranean climate, and the physical security provided by the most ubiquitous police force outside of the Iron Curtain. . . The typical resident and his or her dog (they all seem to have dogs) takes advantage of the abundance of diversions (golf, tennis, jazz festivals, opera, theatre, movies, restaurants, tax-free luxury goods, abundant financial and investment services). As might be expected, the things that wealthy people consider necessities are available in abundance: Health Clubs, Country Clubs, Golf and Tennis Clubs, helicopters, yachts and Lear Jets (buy or hire). Monte Carlo has the largest Rolls and Cadillac dealerships in Europe. There is a large selection of veterinarians of course, plus human medical specialists of all types and a fine new hospital, "The Princess Grace". In the "suburbs" you'll find a sports stadium, beach club, representative offices for most major banks, gourmet restaurants, caterers and delicatessens. With a population of 30,000 and a tiny physical space, Monaco has all the services and cultural activities of a city the size of San Francisco. The reason is that besides the wealthy population, there are normally another half million tourists in the area. They arrive in yachts of all sizes, by train, with tour busses, and by private car. Monaco is convenient for a one or two day visit from most places in Europe. The changing of the guard at the Prince's Palace, while a bit hokey compared to the ritual at Buckingham Palace, is a required stop for millions of tourists each year. The babble of visitors' voices is in a hundred languages. French is the official language but the majority of residents and workers are probably now Italian. For those who don't know Italy and Italians except through movies about the Mafia, look again; the Monaco Italians are a different breed — from the North, not from Sicily. Many are blond, blue-eyed. They dress in fashions that will be popular in New York, Paris or Tokyo next year! Many are rich, very rich. They have class and style, but somewhere along the way these elegant Italians have got the idea that anyone who speaks American English is someone special. As a result, they are exceptionally friendly to English speakers. It's a pleasure to be liked and smiled at! Of course in Monaco, the American Princess Grace was loved. She brought in her friends from Philadelphia's Main Line and from Hollywood. She helped transform Monaco from a place that was going to seed into the fashionable resort it is today. To be a rich American in Monaco was to be "in". It was considered very classy to speak English ever since Princess Grace arrived. That situation still prevails today; anyone with independent means and a modicum of charm will soon have many friends and invitations in Monaco. The official language is French. Most everyone speaks English, Italian and probably German too.

Here's the local "in joke" in Monte Carlo: WHAT IS A MONACAN? An Italian who speaks French and pretends to be an American!

PHYSICAL DESCRIPTION

The Principality of Monaco is a densely populated city-state only two square kilometers in area. Viewed from a helicopter, Monaco and the overlapping City of Monte Carlo appear as a patch of hi-rise apartment buildings sprouting incongruously on a long coastline — otherwise populated by gracious vacation homes. Monaco is built on a slope, going back only four blocks from the sea. On the north it merges into the typical French town of Beausoleil. To the east, small romantic coastal resort towns nudge into each other, crowding the sea in a 100 kilometer stretch of urbanity that goes to Genoa (Italy). To the west is Nice (with its international airport) followed by Antibes and Cannes. The area has been a fashionable resort ever since Queen Victoria and the Russian Tsar built vacation homes there.

Monaco itself is divided into several districts or neighborhoods. "The Rock" is where the old fortress and Prince's Palace are found. It is considered prestigious to live there, but the buildings are mainly medieval, meaning that they are crammed inside what was once a fortress, without a lot of light and air. Of course, the better properties on the outer periphery, with splendid views, can sell for over a million dollars when they (rarely) come on the market. To the west of the Rock is a new neighborhood, Fontvielle, now under construction on landfill. At Fontvielle you'll find a new yacht harbor, the exquisite Princess Grace Rose Garden, and an attractive planned community of nautically oriented high-rise apartments. The least expensive studio in this area would be about F*f*750,000. The same studio would rent for about F*f*32,500 per month on a three year lease. To the east of the Rock is the "Condomine" neighborhood — the old harbor area where there are many small stores, supermarkets, restaurants. One of the battleship-sized yachts in the harbor has "his and her" helicopters perched fore and aft. A few blocks further east is the area known as Monte Carlo. That's the fashionable strolling area with the Casino, Loew's Hotel, the famous Hermitage Hotel and the main park. Many exclusive art galleries and shops, auction houses are found here. Between Monte Carlo and the area to the east of it is the desirable residential section. The best address is "Avenue Princess Grace". Another park, the beach, convention centre, and the Sporting Club are all on this street. On Avenue Princess Grace are the best apartment buildings in town — most of them deluxe rental units going at $2,000 per month and up. They are almost all owned by the wealthiest family in Monaco, the Pastores.

IS MONACO YOUR CUP OF TEA?

Most countries do not tax those of their citizens who live abroad. The United States and the Philippines are the only exceptions. Thus Americans or Filipinos must change passports before being able to take full advantage of a tax haven. The advantages of Monaco include an absence of direct (income) tax, real estate taxes, and inheritance estate taxes where the heirs are spouses or direct descendants. As a result, the people who would benefit from Monaco residence are:

RETIRED OR SEMI-RETIRED HIGH NET WORTH INDIVIDUALS whose incomes derive from assets and investments that can easily be moved (or kept) in havens for capital such as London, New York, or Switzerland. Funds managed in such places can grow without attracting any taxes. Because of French interference, Monaco residents should of course not keep their major assets in Monaco.

ACTIVE, SELF-EMPLOYED INDIVIDUALS WHOSE INCOMES ARE NOT TIED TO BEING IN SOME OTHER LOCATION ON A PERMANENT BASIS. Financial consultants, artists, writers, sports and show business personalities, fashion designers. These are a few of the self-employed categories who find Monaco an attractive base.

PEOPLE WHO LIKE THE RIVIERA enough to spend at least six months a year there.

Obviously, a first consideration is whether you have enough wealth or earnings to justify the expense and inconvenience of moving to a new location with probably higher living costs, and the need for making certain adjustments in language, leisure time activities, and way of life.

It is possible that you would like Monaco so much that even without the tax haven feature you should consider moving there. But assuming that the tax considerations are important, the question becomes: "Does the money I save on taxes make it financially worth while to move?" Obviously, the majority of rich New Yorkers stay in New York, despite high Federal, State and Local taxes. Perhaps it is because they don't know any better! Perhaps they make more money (even after taxes) than they would if they lost their daily contacts and personal information sources. More likely the truth is that even highly taxed, wealthy people stay put because inertia is very strong. The forceful kick of some unacceptable new tax or law is necessary before any move is seriously considered. A close relative of mine lived and died in one of the worst places on Earth. His city was dull, boring, polluted, crime-ridden. It had a horrible climate, and had nothing to recommend it. He could have afforded to move at anytime. His business would have prospered even more elsewhere. Why didn't he leave? I asked him many times. The answer was "This is my home." "Why couldn't somewhere else be your home? You always complain about your tax problems and the lack of interesting, stimulating friends." He answered: "At least I know what my problems are here." This individual was afraid of the unknown. Like most people, he was resistant to change of any kind — even if it meant an improvement. Successful entrepreneurs, successful people in general have a different mentality. They go where the sun shines brightest — where the economic climate affords them maximum opportunity to realize their goals. For many rich retired Italians, Monaco is not much of a move. They remain a few minutes drive from the favorite chain-stores, restaurants, relatives. They can tune into the favorite radio and television stations and read their usual daily papers. They can speak their own language since everyone in Monaco speaks Italian, French, and usually English as well. For the Italian, a move to Monte Carlo is like a New Yorker retiring to join his old cronies in Tucson, Arizona.

An American or English person in Monaco has a slightly greater culture shock to contend with, but the Anglo community is about 2,000 strong. With another five to ten thousand English speaking tourists in town on any given day, there is no shortage of English language newspapers, magazines, hamburgers, movies, and even USA television channels that bring (via satellite) all the familiar programs. The telephone operators and postal clerks speak English. The level of personal services is just as good as, if not better than in London or New York. Certainly the streets are cleaner, the public parks more well tended, and the degree of personal safety much higher.

The weather in Monaco is good about eight months a year. It seldom freezes, but January through March tend to be drizzly and overcast. It is however only a short drive to the most popular ski resorts of the French and Swiss Alps; these being in high season at this time. During the winter, older residents tend to put their cars on a ferry to the sunshine of Morocco or Israel. Still others will board one of the many cruise ships that depart from nearby Nice for the Caribbean or South America.

The opportunity for making a good living in Monaco is present, but there are limitations. Unemployment is high all over Europe. Sales-related work in stockbrokerage, banking, insurance, financial management, yacht-sales is usually available to those who can produce enough business to cover their draws. Self-employed individuals in categories not requiring a professional license can do well — dance and yoga teachers, hang-gliding experts, tennis professionals, etc. Americans are considered a bit exotic, open-handed, friendly and honest, and are generally well received. They tend to be more socially mobile and employable than Europeans, who are pigeon-holed into certain categories because of their accents or the schools they attended.

As might be expected there are a vast number of social and athletic clubs that one can join. These cater to every conceivable interest. There are religious congregations of every faith. Every ethnic group seems to be represented. There are a few hundred Asians and Arabs, but these tend to be the smallest ethnic groups. Dues at the most elite organizations (Monte Carlo Country Club, etc.) are quite a bit lower than one would expect, as are tickets to the many charity balls. These low prices I discovered reflect the fact that taxpayers can deduct most of the expense or have a company pay it in New York or London. But where there are no taxes, prices reflect supply and demand. Thus a $500 a plate dinner for the New York Museum of Modern Art might be only F*f*250 for the Monegasque equivalent.

AVAILABLE SINGLE MEN, WOMEN

As might be expected with a population that could be described as two-thirds retired or independently wealthy, there is a predominance of wealthy widows over sixty years of age who seem to be quite happy with a social life invariably including the constant companionship of their lap dogs. The most beautiful young and available women in the world seem to spend their summers, bare breasted, at the beach, pools and gaming tables. Single older men of independent means as a result seem to have a good time, whether with rich widows or young swingers. There is a small gay community, and a few bars and clubs catering to this group (both male and female). An individual with anything to offer should have no trouble in making friends. English and American singles tend to drop in at the Flashman's Pub and the hotel bars. The Yachting set congregate at the many bars and restaurants near the old harbor. The beach and beachside restaurants as well as the disco at the Sporting Club are other friendly places for the young to middle aged. Affinity or special interest clubs are the best bet for the over 65s. A list of groups and meeting times can be obtained from the Tourist Information office near the Old Casino. Because of the transient population, people tend to be friendly, always looking for replacements for those friends who have moved on. If one gets involved in charity work, it is not hard to meet the most elite members of Monaco society. These will include a selection of Barons, Dukes, Earls, Princesses, and just plain millionaires.

HOW TO BECOME A LEGAL RESIDENT

The first step is to apply to the nearest French Consulate for a resident's visa, specifying Monaco as the place of intended residence. The French Consulate will supply the necessary application forms in response to a letter, telephone call, or personal visit. The Consulate may request any or all of the following:

A. A letter or other document from the Police Department of your present residence giving details of your criminal record, if any. Obviously a "clean record" will not present any barriers. A record of convictions might cause delay or denial particularly if the offenses are considered serious matters by the French or Monegasque authorities.

B A bankers's letter certifying that your assets and income will allow you to live in Monaco without gainful employment. At the present time it is not necessary in most cases to give anyone a detailed financial statement. The Consul merely wants to verify that you have enough to live on. About F*f*30,000 per month would be the minimum income. There is no hard and fast rule, however.

C A list of personal possessions, appliances (including cars) that will be brought into France and/or Monaco. The Consul will certify this list, and the items thereon will be admitted duty free. Note: Cars must have been owned for over a year.

D A medical examination certificate, translated into French may be required by the Consul, but he doesn't always ask for one. It definitely will be required in Monaco when you turn in a prior driving license and receive (without examination) a Monaco driving license, good for life.

WORK PERMITS

The residence permit (without a work permit) will be issued in one to three months. A work permit request will probably hold up the application unless an employer in Monaco certifies that a job is waiting, and has been approved by the Monaco Labour Office. Entrepreneurial activity, personal trading in stocks or commodities, investing in local real estate, being a fashion designer, artist, writer etc. does not require a work permit or license. Highly paid self-employed individuals are welcomed, so long as what they do does not take away employment from locals.

You can visit Monaco and purchase or rent an apartment without a residence permit, so long as you leave the country at least once every three months and have an address elsewhere. You need never become officially registered as a resident. However in order to prove to the prior country of residence that you have indeed moved, (if that is necessary or desirable) many individuals will get the Monaco Resident's Identification Card. But remember the "permanent tourist" option we discussed earlier. You can have maximum privacy and freedom by having no official domicile. If one gets the residence permit without the right to work first it is relatively easy to get a work permit in Monaco at a later date. Of course, this will only be for the type of activities that are considered "proper" for Monaco.

THE MONACO IDENTIFICATION CARD

This document (a considerable status symbol in Europe) looks much like a plastic credit card with your picture on it. It is issued by the Monaco Police Station or prefecture located in the Condomine or "Old Harbor" area. In order to obtain it, one visits the police station with what they call a "record of punishments", i.e., police record from your prior residence, the banker's letter certifying that you have sufficient income to support yourself without working, your passport containing a French Residential Visa. Last but not least, you'll need a copy of THE RESIDENTIAL LEASE OR CERTIFICATE OF OWNERSHIP for an apartment in Monaco. It is a good idea also to bring in at this time your old driving license and car title.

Your photograph is taken during this visit. You will be assisted in applying for your driving license (for which you must have a medical certificate showing fitness). If you have owned a car over a year, and agree not to sell it for another two years, you will get Monaco car license plates and registration documents at a nominal charge. On a new car, there might be a duty of up to 35% of value.

That is all there is to it! Once in Monaco, if you want to start a business or get a job, if you or the business are not considered "undesirable" arrangements can usually be made. It may be a good idea to employ a local lawyer or "Notaire" to assist with arrangements, particularly if you don't speak French.

Citizenship is difficult to obtain. One will not even be given the application forms until at least ten years after taking up residence. Unless you are a large scale public benefactor, you can forget about a Monegasque passport.

GOVERNMENT

Monaco is a constitutional monarchy presided over by the same Grimaldi family for over 500 years. Because of its small size, Monaco has always been a protectorate subject to a powerful neighboring state. The degree of sovereignty has varied considerably over time. The relationship with France dates back to 1793 when it was swallowed up. Independence was granted twenty years later. In 1963 France forced Monaco into subordination to Paris on all matters involving money, exchange controls, banking and customs. French nationals living in Monaco were made subject to French taxes and military service. But native Monegasques and foreigners were exempt.

Monaco was forced to submit to all French indirect taxes (most notably, the TVA or 33% value added tax), and economic controls. France collects and rebates taxes on a revenue sharing basis. This proved to be a windfall for Monaco. Previously the Casino had provided most revenues. Today the state owned casinos provide under 10% of state revenue.

Although many wealthy French scattered like frightened ducks, after 1963 they were replaced by Italians. As to local affairs, there is an elected council of eighteen members who govern under the executive power of the Prince and the Minister of State. **A 1918 treaty with France provides that should the Grimaldi dynasty die out, Monaco will revert to France.** The Minister of State who controls the licensing of business activities must be French. Monaco is entirely dependent upon French systems for all utilities. This means that mail is delivered twice a day, water and electricity are priced reasonably and phones generally work.

Most of the 25,000 wealthy foreigners keep only some pin money in Monaco banks. As a result, bank deposits per inhabitant in Monaco average over $75,000. This compares with about $3,000 per person in the rest of France. Besides attracting all this money into the French banking system, another advantage to France in maintaining the status quo is that Monte Carlo provides an outlet for luxury goods and fashion products. Thus it provides a showcase for "the best of France". If France withdrew the remaining privileges of Monaco, it would lose this small group of very wealthy consumers and trend setters. Besides the wealthy widows and retired business men, Monaco attracts talented and productive people who have in the past added to the lustre, glory and prestige of France. Without the tax exemptions they could easily move to Bermuda, Portofino, Campione, Bahamas or Hong Kong and continue their present tax-free lifestyle. French politicians apparently think they have more to lose than to gain by taking over this small enclave and scattering its residents to other tax havens. Unfortunately, leftist politicians seldom promote rational economic policies and Monaco residents, like wealthy foreigners everywhere, prudently keep their big money out of French control. Beside keeping their money abroad, they have a second home available in nearby Italy in case Monaco becomes untenable. For the time being however, Monaco is perhaps the best tax haven in the world to live in.

A BIT OF HISTORY

The public relations releases of Monaco seldom mention it, but the year 1963 was a turning point in Monegasque history. Before that time Monaco was more independent. Taxes for all were very low, and income taxes, then as now, were nonexistent. Revenues from the gambling casino funded the limited municipal services (police, fire protection, roads). Because pre-war taxes in France were low or easily evaded, Monaco's main attraction was not the low taxes, but rather its scenic harbor location, the casino, and relatively mild winter climate. It was a decidedly sleepy enclave, much like Campione is today. During the Euro-boom of the post-war 1950s, several factors caused Monaco's emergence as a personal tax haven. Taxes in France rose dramatically to pay for war reconstruction, foreign military actions, and expanded social programs. The French tax collector's voracious appetites were accompanied by more efficient methods of collection and enforcement. These included occasional criminal penalties to make examples of offenders with Swiss bank accounts who could be portrayed as egregious examples of tax evasion and fraud. Of course, the socialist politicians soon ran up against the "Laffer Curve". Although undiscovered and un-named at the time, this economic law is that as tax rates rise, collections diminish. Instead of transferring wealth, high tax rates eventually only transfer taxpayers. Many French industrialists simply moved themselves and their operating headquarters to Monaco, New York or Geneva where their books and banking activities were safe from the prying eyes of the French Revenuers. France hit back. What happened in Geneva and New York are not part of this story. In Monaco however, the local government was in 1963 simply forced at virtual gunpoint to give in to French demands that its tax system be aligned with that of France in respect to all French companies and individuals in Monaco. France of course had the military power to terminate Monaco entirely, but it saw fit to allow non-French individuals to avoid both French and their home country's taxes. Perhaps this was a way of getting back at England, USA and Italy which were then attracting too many wealthy French by offering tax and other concessions. The 1963 agreement provided for an alignment of indirect taxes, customs and excises, gasoline taxes, and currency controls. Taxes were collected by France, and a portion remitted back to the Monaco Government. A very few exceptions were allowed in order to keep some of its *raison d'etre* (reason to exist) as an attraction for the vacationing international set. One such exemption was on valuable antiques and jewellery. They can still be sold with considerably less tax than in France. But low priced groceries, liquor, gasoline and tobacco would never again attract great masses of day-trippers to Monaco, as they still do in Andorra and the Channel Islands.

Grace Kelly, the American movie star who became Princess Grace, is given much credit for working out the new economic plan that after the 1963 debacle was to cause Monaco to become the world's most elegant tax haven. The idea was to discourage mass tourism or cheap vacation packages and concentrate upon making Monaco a centre for the very wealthy. As it turned out, France contributed unexpectedly high revenues as Monaco's share of the new tax take. As the stream of French tax avoiders petered out, wealthy Italians moved in. A convention centre, hospital and stadium were built along with the two new casinos. Five Star hotels and thousands of high-rise condominium apartments went up. To avoid the appearance of giving haven to "tax abusers" Monaco insisted that any legal residents who wished to take advantage of the lack of income tax must actually stay in Monaco six months per year. (This way a resident will presumably support the local economy by paying the indirect taxes upon purchases of household necessities, visiting the Casino, enjoying local entertainments, etc.) Naturally with so many wealthy, often elderly residents, Monaco could have become a favorite of confidence men, jewel thieves, financial sharpies and others who could prey upon the local population. To prevent this Monaco installed electronic surveillance, and registration procedures that have made the country into what many people term a "mini-police state". **There are more police officers per resident in Monaco than in any other country in the world.** However, the tight control by these white gloved, exceedingly polite gentlemen who will actually salute you, is not there to diminish the freedom of the residents, but to protect them and their way of life. The majority of Monaco residents have absolutely no political voice, but that is the bargain you'll have to make when moving to Monaco: Accept the status quo. "If you don't like it, go somewhere else" is the clear message to foreigners who get political. Monaco extends the welcome mat to individuals or companies of prestige, good reputation and wealth, not political activists. The cost of living is high, but steep prices are the price of admission for an environment with plenty of glitter and action. Jazz festivals, art auctions, charity balls, first class night-club revues, championship golf and tennis tournaments, the Grand Prix auto race — all these events follow one another in a succession of glamorous diversions. It is possible to live on a starvation budget in Monaco, but that is not the reason anyone comes here.

WHAT'S NOT GOOD ABOUT MONACO

Assume that one likes the many glamorous diversions that Monaco offers, what are the negatives?

Being subject to French currency controls is one problem. Fortunately assets left outside of Monaco are exempt and need not be reported. For two years after arrival even local bank accounts are exempted. *Thus exchange controls are entirely avoided by simply keeping your assets out of Monaco.*

The lack of constipated dogs is immediately apparent to anyone attempting to walk the streets of Monaco. I personally do not own a dog or want one. But most retired people seem to like dogs, and the most visible presence in Monaco seems to be canine. The police do not enforce any politeness on the part of dogs, and thus they commit nuisances every few meters along the public walkways. For Americans who may not understand this delicate euphemism, an alternative title considered for this Report was, "Monaco, Principality of Poop". Since passage through Monaco is often accomplished on foot through beautifully lit marble lined subterranean corridors and a system of public elevators, the presence of so much excrement among so much luxury is extremely offensive, particularly indoors, in confined spaces. But dog lovers do not seem to mind it. After a few weeks one learns to cope by watching one's step, and avoiding the malodorous underground passageways, despite their convenience.

The high cost of rent and real estate may be a complaint for some, but they are not out of line for what you get. Living in an exclusive neighborhood can never be cheap. If it were, the neighborhood would no longer be exclusive. A decent one bedroom apartment can be rented for *f*3,000 per month.

Monaco is of course crowded. But it is the crowds of wealthy people who support the fine restaurants and entertainment. Only in August does Monaco become as unbearable as rush hour on the Tokyo subway. Yet the mobs who visit in August are not forced to be there. Obviously, they like the crush of high season on the Riviera. In contrast, from January to March, Monaco's apartment buildings seem to be empty except for concierges at the desks. During winter, Monaco weather is generally slightly above freezing and often rainy. The entire Riviera is pretty dead. But you can still swim at several elegant indoor pools — and work-out at Loew's or the California Terrace Health Club. Hotels offer 50% discounts from the high season, and manage to limp along, helped by investment and sales conferences that keep occupancy rates at 75%. The Loew's Casinos are always full of customers. The Sporting Club closes for the winter.

POLITICAL STABILITY

During the recent leftist Mitterand administration in France, there were no changes within Monaco. But, it must be recognized that Monaco's stability and very existence is only due to the tolerance of France. France imposed a wealth tax (in France) a few years ago that fell heavily upon owners of second homes in the French Riviera. This tax sent values (outside of Monaco) plummeting by 75%. Prior to the high taxes, foreigners resident in Monaco and wealthy Monegasques invariably owned a large country estate and a few acres of ground in nearby France or Italy. This enabled them to escape the congestion of Monaco on weekends, and to enjoy a bit of gardening, fresh country air and perhaps tennis or swimming at their private facilities. But Socialist France was determined to end a life of "privilege", even for the foreigners in their midst, and **the new laws were applied even to foreigners** who owned vacation homes in France. As a result, the once universal practice of having a small apartment in Monaco and a sprawling mansion at nearby Cap Ferrat, Cap St. Martin, or Cap D'Antibes is undergoing a process of change. The larger homes are being sold and divided up into condominium apartments.

The future of Monaco depends upon the protection and patronage of France. Some have compared the Monaco/France situation to the relationship between Hong Kong and China. The Monte Carlo administration realizes the delicacy of its position and does all it can to accommodate France. They will give France no reason to take away the limited remaining sovereignty. It must be recognized that some unpredictable event could result in the incorporation of Monaco into France at any time. In San Marino (a similar one-time tax haven enclave in Italy), overspending by the local government precipitated a national insolvency a few years ago. This was resolved by Rome taking away San Marino's traditional privileges: no more casino, no more independent radio or TV stations, no more tax haven. The immediate result was that most of the population of San Marino emigrated to the USA. San Marino was left with an ultra-leftist Communist repressive regime that was compared to Albania. What could happen in Monaco is anyone's guess. But the ruling Grimaldi family has handled relations with France skilfully since the debacle of 1963, and young Prince Albert (the heir apparent) seems to have been trained to carry out the conservative, accommodating policies of his father, Prince Rainer. These have resulted in incredible development and prosperity for the little Principality.

TO BUY OR TO RENT?

The big question mark, "What will the French do?" causes most foreign expatriates in Monaco to keep substantial assets invested elsewhere. Only long term residents buy apartments to enjoy the appreciation in values and avoid the annual rent increases. Both have averaged 6% (in Francs) for many years.

Monaco has a reasonable form of rent control that allows annual increases based upon the percentage increase in the cost of construction. This has not proved to be a burden to rental property owners. There is a healthy occupancy rate of about 98%. Accordingly only overpriced or inferior apartments are vacant for long. Because of the ageing population, there are always a number of good apartments coming available for rent or for sale. The net return on investment in apartments averages 5% per annum. New construction, particularly in the land-fill area of Fontvielle is providing a large number of modern units for which it will be necessary to attract new immigrants. This area is now dusty and full of unpleasant building activity. But when complete, by 1992, Fontvielle will be an attractive planned community with a modern harbor, heliport, and high level facilities. Although apartments across the French border sell for about half the prices in Monaco, the expense of *f*750,000 and up for a studio apartment may be justified. Mortgage financing is available, but generally loan pay-offs or renegotiations are required every five years. There are very few freehold homes in Monaco — perhaps a few dozen. Two or three are always on the market. The prices for a "so-so" villa without a view seem to start at 10 million francs. A similar home in France can be acquired for f2,500,000. Despite the taxes in France, the French home seems a better investment since the earnings on *f*10 million would pay the taxes 100 times over. But because of France's past shabby treatment of wealthy foreign property owners, nearby Italy would be my choice for a comfortable country estate, if I could not resist the temptation to buy something. But remember, in Italy, there is a hefty capital gains tax enforced against foreigners. This tax may be exorbitant because Italian sellers always insist upon half their sales price being paid "under the table." The result is that a substantial paper gain on sale may attract a much higher tax than is actually warranted. Also, both Italy and France (as of 1988) still have exchange controls making it difficult to get house-sale proceeds out of the country. Many people regret their purchases. No one can make a mistake by renting.

The customary residential lease in Monaco is for three years. A deposit of the first two months and last two months rent is not uncommon. There may also be a large "utility and charges" deposit equal to six months estimated heat and power. "Key Money" is another item often requested, especially when the unexpired portion of someone else's lease is being taken over. In France, key money reflects the difference between the rent controlled price and fair market value capitalized over twenty years. It could run to $100,000 or more on a luxury unit. In Monaco, where rents tend to be at market level, key money represents whatever the prior tenant can convince you his built-in appliances and improvements are worth. The typical unfurnished apartment in Monaco comes *without* sink, stove, kitchen cabinets, refrigerator, washer, dryer, closet fittings, bookshelves, carpets, drapes or light fixtures. In the dozens of apartments personally viewed by this author, the key money requested ran from a minimum of $1,000 up to $25,000 for a fully furnished, nicely done two bedroom model.

When going for your resident's card it is necessary to show a "registered" lease. The cost of registering a lease is 1% of the 3 year term. Thus if the rent is *f*3,000 per month, registration is *f*1,080 (3,000 x 36 x .01) extra. Incidentally, it is impossible for a landlord to evict a tenant who pays rent and is not a public nuisance.

GARAGE SPACE — CARS — PERSONAL TRANSPORTATION

Obtaining your own off street parking spot is necessary, particularly in the summer months. There are a number of public underground garages where monthly spaces can be rented for around $30 per month. A "box" or closed (lockable) parking space can be purchased for about F100,000, or rented privately from between *f*250 and *f*350 per month. French francs are the unit of currency in Monaco.

It is possible to get along without a car in Monaco as local and intercity bus and train service is very frequent and convenient. But to enjoy the many country restaurants and to be able to visit friends in the rural areas a car is nice to have. Of course Hertz, Avis, Eurocar all have large fleets in Monaco. You can rent when needed. Many individuals cope with difficult parking and congestion problems by getting a small motorcycle as their main or auxiliary personal transport. Because of the hills a bicycle is a rather exhausting way to get around Monaco. Public buses are better.

Taxis or rental limousines with uniformed drivers are also available from about $15 per hour on up.

United States made cars are increasingly rare in Europe, but there is a large General Motors agency as well as Europe's major Rolls-Royce/Ferrari/Porsche sales and service in Monaco. Mercedes, Renault, Citroen, Fiat are the most common cars. Unleaded gas is very hard to find except at the autoroute stations outside of town. Diesel fuel is plentiful and much cheaper than gasoline (particularly in Italy). Gasoline in Europe tends to be triple the USA cost. Due to the constricted, winding roads, parking difficulties, and difficulties in selling big cars, the largest practical cars to own are the "baby" Benz (Model 190 Mercedes, about *f*120,000 tax free) or the BMW 320, slightly cheaper. For those who don't need prestige cars, Fiats (Uno and Panda) are Europe's best sellers. Japanese cars in France and Italy are rare, service facilities for them are few and far between. The best place to buy a tax-free car in Europe is from any factory authorized dealer in Copenhagen, Denmark. You get license plates good for two years, and the lowest list prices in the world on all makes of cars. These cars can be used all over Europe until the license expires. Then they can be re-licensed tax-free in Monaco. A new Porsche for instance could be acquired in this way for under US $14,000 (as of 1988).

REGISTRATION AND TRANSFER TAXES — Buying Real Estate in Monaco

In Monaco (also in France, Italy and Spain) Americans and English people will be pleased to discover that real estate taxes are almost non-existent. They will be less happy to note that upon purchase or sale of property in these same countries, there is a substantial charge for selling or making transfers. In Monaco, when real estate is sold, gifted or inherited, the costs of registering the transfer will be about 7.5% for the State, 3% for a Notaire, and 3% to 6% for the real estate agencies handling the deal. With up to 16% in add-on charges for a buyer (and some other charges for the seller), it is hard to make any quick profits by trading real estate. For someone experienced in these transactions, costs can be reduced by one or all of the following means:

1. Acquiring a newly built apartment as the first occupant. In these situations the price is usually "net" with the seller paying all the closing costs. If he doesn't, you can refuse to buy. Always bargain for the best deal. Even "fixed prices" are flexible.
2. Acquiring property in the name of a foreign holding company. The same company remains the owner both before and after the transaction where the buyer takes possession of "bearer shares".

If the seller is dishonest and the holding company has undisclosed debts you may have problems. But otherwise, there is no change of ownership as far as the State is concerned.

3. It is apparently common for a notaire to reduce the stated price of an apartment or home by raising the value of the furnishings or other means. If you have a reputable notaire, be guided by his advice as to the usual manner in which things are handled. You would not wish to start off your Monaco residence in a manner that would bring you unwelcome official attention.

4. Properties may be bought directly from sellers who post notices on the HAVAS bulletin board near the Casino, or advertise in the several free advertising papers distributed at the Tourist Office. There are also ads in the local daily papers such as Nice-Matin. The Herald Tribune also often has ads for Monaco properties. The Wall Street Journal has a Monaco section every few months. Bankers and word-of-mouth leads often result in real estate deals that are much better than the properties listed with agents. The best policy is to start off by renting an apartment in Monaco short-term. Or stay in a hotel for several weeks while you explore. There does not seem to be any seasonal variation in prices, but the market hibernates during the winter months. Everything looks the worst, and gloomy weather may make some owners anxious to sell.

OPERATING A BUSINESS IN MONACO

Informal operations that can be managed from one's apartment, and without permanent staff are ideal for Monaco. Low profile consultants, artists, creative people in general, authors for instance, are untaxed, unregulated. In my opinion they are best advised to remain unregistered. The government wishes to attract business ventures of prestige that are neither labor-intensive nor a source of public nuisance. All such operations must be approved by the Minister of State, and generally three years of prior profitable operations must be demonstrated. The official tax rate on profits is 35%, but most enterprises can legally avoid taxes by properly structuring the business. The effective cost of setting up and running an enterprise from Monaco then is reduced to the cost of incorporating and hiring local accountants and lawyers. Renting approved office space is required, but commercial rents tend to be reasonable. Taxes payable to the State are typically a small percentage of office running expenses. The State has the right to withdraw a license at anytime for breaches of approved conduct. Non-Monegasque citizens can't expect much "justice" after a government order to quit the principality.

Unfavorable publicity, criminal indictments or accusations of fraud are likely to bring about a speedy expulsion from Monaco. There is no judicial review and the operation of any business (and residence permission itself) is at the absolute discretion of the government. Normally, a local lawyer will keep an "honest businessman" out of trouble with the government. Typical businesses operating out of Monaco and paying an effective 3% tax, include the chartering of ships, insurance, management of foreign companies or foreign-based investments, finance of motion pictures and light manufacturing in Monaco (computer chips, pharmaceuticals, jewellery, and high-fashion) commodity and security trading, real estate holdings.

Most Monaco banks will advise and assist potential customers with setting up and operating a business in compliance with local laws. Robert Rouker, Vice-President of CITIBANK, Box 165, MC6800, Monaco, has a fourteen page technical booklet explaining the details of Monaco incorporation and business operations. The bottom line is that business operations considered desirable will be given the red carpet treatment, and will suffer little harassment, inspection or taxation. Sharp operators and fraudsters will get a rough escort to the border.

INHERITANCE AND ESTATE TAXES: PROBATES AND ESTATE ADMINISTRATION

Only assets situated within the Principality are subject to estate duties. For those in a direct line (parents, children or spouses) the tax is zero regardless of the amount involved. Bequests or inheritances to brothers and sisters are taxed at 8%; uncles, aunts, nephews, nieces — 10%; other blood relatives 13%; unrelated parties or foreign charities — 16%.

Negotiable securities held by local banks are subject to inheritance taxes. It is possible to set up and administer trusts from Monaco. There are trust companies, and the charges and .02% annual tax are similar to the bank charges in Liechtenstein or the Channel Islands, where most wealthy individuals prefer to have their testamentary affairs administered. Author's note: Because of French exchange controls, and the possiblity of United Kingdom controls in the Channel Islands, a Liechtenstein Foundation remains the best option for managing a family fortune for the benefit of heirs who are too young or incompetent to be given the assets directly. For estates involving over $750,000, the author will be glad to assist in arranging for testamentary disposition that will avoid taxes, exchange controls, estate or probate administration costs, and the possibility of squabbling between the heirs. My fee would include a consultation on how best to manage assets during your lifetime.

The laws of Monaco, like the laws of France, curtail the power of an individual to disinherit children or grandchildren. Considerable formalities are required to make a valid will in Monaco. Well advised individuals in most cases should keep their apartment (if owned) in the name of an "offshore" bearer-share corporation or Liechtenstein foundation, and only a small local bank account for current expenses. The family car, if expensive, should also be in the name of the Liechtenstein company. A trustee could then (in the event of death) take over and dispose of all assets without the registration and transfer fees and taxes (of around 10%) that would otherwise be necessary. The costs of a Liechtenstein foundation would be around $3,000 to set up and $1,000 per year to administer.

THE QUESTION MARK (?)

Why, I wondered, would anyone in their right mind move to the Island of Jersey when instead of their 20% flat rate income tax and requirements of full financial disclosure, one could have zero taxes in the other popular tax havens. Why should anyone pay upwards of $600,000 for Jersey housing when even in expensive Monaco, a seafront apartment could be purchased for half that price?

And if one was so enamoured with the terrible damp, sub-zero winter winds of the English Channel, why not rent or buy a short distance away in *Sark* where a home, fifty to a hundred acres of land, a seat in Parliament, and *zero taxes* could all be had for half the price of just an ordinary house in Jersey?

Jersey has a few more stores, and an airport. But the regular hydrofoils from Sark get you to Jersey or Guernsey very quickly.

The answer is that not many people do actually opt for Jersey or Guernsey in comparison with Monaco. And in speaking with those who do, the only answer seemed to be that for some people in England, the Channel Islands had become "status symbols". People buy terrible cars at exhorbitant prices because they are status symbols. Rolls, Lamborghini and Maserati cars for instance, are worthless, except for impressing someone. I feel the same way about Jersey as a tax haven!

WHEN TO COME AND WHEN TO GO

August and to a lesser extent July are the high-season months in Monaco. If you own an apartment, these months will command rents of four times normal. If crowds are your thing, this could be the most enjoyable time of the year for you. The small beach, the restaurants, the Casino — all are jam-packed. There are many events of interest to tourists along the entire Riviera.

For an active and busy time with plenty of scheduled activities and entertainments, April - May - June and September - October - November would be my choice. You can find a parking place and eat at most restaurants without reservations during these months. The weather is at its best.

December - January - February are good months to get away from the drizzles and cold by moving to your digs in Palm Beach, Florida or Palm Desert, California. Of course the South American and Australia-New Zealand summers are on. The beaches of Bali or Thailand offer a sunny contrast to the always depressing European winter. One can take a cruise to the Caribbean, or drive to the desert resorts near Eilat, Israel.

Ain't life grand when the most major decision you are confronted with is "Where shall we spend the winter?"

For many individuals, the tax savings afforded by a move to Monaco may make such a life reality instead of a dream!

TRANSPORTATION AND COMMUNICATION

Monaco is a seven minute ride by regular helicopter service to the Nice International Airport. From this airport there are many direct flights to London, Paris, North America, the Middle East, Africa, and the Orient.

Depending on traffic, the limo ride, Nice to Monaco, takes forty minutes to 1½ hours.

The Monaco train station, a regular stop on international trains, is within walking distance from anywhere in Monaco. Trains are far more clean, fast and dependable than in North or South America. They are also generally half the price of inter-European air travel.

Several "Pullman" bus companies serve Monaco and one can take a bus to London or most other cities by direct, express services. Individuals from outside Europe will be surprised at the cleanliness and efficiency of these services. Buses are slightly cheaper than trains.

Monaco is located on the European freeway system, and upon entering the toll road system at Monaco, you can then drive without speed limits or stop lights all the way to Rome, Vienna, Paris, Milan or Hamburg without a stop. Freeway service stations are open 24 hours per day, every day. Many "Autoroute" stations offer a choice of lead free, high octane super, regular, diesel and propane fuels.

TELEPHONES/TELEX/FAX/MAIL

The service is French and thus pretty good. France has recently introduced the futuristic "Minitel" or computer-phone that can be used for electronic mail, shopping, banking, stock trading, etc. It is subsidized by the government. You get the screen and keyboard "free", paying only for the facilities you use.

TELEVISION/RADIO

Monaco has independent commercial radio and television stations broadcasting in Italian and French. K.O.S.T. radio, a local station based in nearby Mortola, Italy, broadcasts in English. The BBC and Communists also can be heard in English every evening on short wave. FM stations broadcast mainly "American Top 40" and considerable classical music, the best classical being found on Radio Tre (Italy). The better hotels and apartment buildings have satellite receptors that bring in dozens of TV channels from all over the world.

As a result of some additional personal experience in Monaco this year, we are passing on the following information, new for 1988-89.

REAL ESTATE BROKERS IN MONACO

Monaco must be as over-populated by licensed real estate agents as is California. There, one out of every ten adults is reportedly in the business. You will have no trouble finding brokers on the main commercial streets. Several are a little bit "special". We want to comment about them:

John R. Taylor & Co. specializes in the better, more expensive properties around the Riviera. They have many offices along the coast in addition to the one in Monaco. If you want to have a look at million-dollar-plus villas and penthouse apartments, they have a selection. They want to show to "qualified buyers". So wear your Rolex, and look rich when you go in for your appointment.

AGEDI 26 bis. Blvd. Princess Charlotte, MC98000, telephone 93.50.66.00 has plenty of expensive properties, but also a wide selection of listings in all price classes. One exceedingly useful service they provide is an extensive (free) print-out of their current listings in each category and price class. For instance, if you want a list of all "studio apartments under F*f*1,000,000 (approximately $160,000)" you could ask for it by mail. Their categories are: APARTMENTS, VILLAS and COMMERCIAL SPACE. Like J.R. Taylor, AGEDI is a big outfit, but it has only one office (in Monaco). They specialize in Monaco and the immediately surrounding area.

Agence Grande Bretagne is a small agency run by Mr Nigro and his attractive (single!) daughter. She is about 25 and speaks fluent English as well as French and Italian. This office takes color photographs of their listings, which makes it possible to save a lot of time by zeroing in on the attractive (to you) properties, while skipping the ugly ducklings. All the agencies in town will have someone who speaks English, so that is not the reason I want to give a special plug to Miss Nigro. She is the only broker in Monaco who came up with a few "bargains" and distress sales due to probates, divorces and so on. She also knows of a few rental deals too. Finally, her grandmother, down the street, owns a different agency. If you want to go through her picture book, you can do that too. The whole family is sincere, patient and honest. They also have some tales to tell about the difficulties (and ultimate success) in obtaining Monaco citizenship. It only takes three(!) generations.

Real Estate Agent in French by the way is "IMMEUBILIER" as opposed to "MEUBILIER", the latter meaning "furniture store". Just in case you forgot, I mentioned earlier that should you acquire a small apartment in Monaco (by renting or buying): if you get tired of the congestion, DO NOT buy a home or agricultural property nearby in France. The French "Fisc" will be after you within three years for taxes on your worldwide income. Italy however, never (up till now) bothers foreigners who don't have a visible business in Italy. You can get a nice country home in the area near Dolche Acqua, Perinaldo, or San Remo — all within half an hour's driving time of Monaco. The prices in Italy are "peanuts" compared with Monaco.

MAKING THE MOST OF MONACO — Summary and Conclusions

An American or Filipino must first change citizenship because those countries will assess "estimated" income taxes when passports are renewed, and merely changing residence does not lead to an exemption from income taxes. (As a practical matter, the problem can be skirted by renewing passports from within the country, or handling the matter several other ways).

A relatively modest apartment can be purchased in Monaco, and the joys of fresh air, quiet, and privacy may be experienced by owning or renting a villa in nearby Italy. Home ownership in France is an invitation to horrendous harassment by the French fiscal authorities, although they take about three years to become a nuisance. One can also rent in Monaco, but on balance a desirable apartment is probably a good investment. Rents from such a unit may be received tax-free. At some future time, if the rules change, it is more likely that property owners in Monaco will be favored under "grandfather clauses" that allow them to retain historic advantages. Even in 1962 when French in Monaco were subjected to all the tax obligations of French residents, those French who had their only home in Monaco for over five years were exempted.

When moving to Monaco, if one desires an expensive car, it should not be purchased in Monaco where ordinary VAT, taxes and dealer mark-ups will double the price. Denmark has the world's lowest auto prices. After one year of ownership, the Danish registration may be transferred to Monaco without substantial tax. All home furnishings and appliances that are wanted in Monaco can and should be purchased abroad at tax-free ports such as Jersey or Singapore. To be eligible for duty-free importation into Monaco, they must be listed upon your visa application as household goods. Items like satellite receptor dishes, computers, television sets, refrigerators, and high-tech non-French made items can be purchased for at least 50% less than in Monaco. The same is true of the best designer label furniture.

Do not apply for a "work-permit" with your initial application. If the type of work you do requires an office and staff, rent your apartment *first,* register with the police as a resident, and retain one of the two or three "notaires" in Monaco to help you get your permit to establish a business. If properly set up by a notaire, the Monaco tax on your business should be about 3% of annual profits, even though the "official tax on business" is 35% of profits.

Do not engage in any political activities or protests; do not get in any disputes with native Monegasques; do not engage in any activities harmful to the reputation of Monaco (frauds, pornography, illicit drug trafficking). If one gets into trouble with the authorities, they can issue a 24 hour notice of expulsion, and there are no effective appeals from this order.

Enjoy yourself in the safest, most prosperous enclave on Earth!

AN INVITATION!

In the event that you move to Monaco partly as a result of reading this Report, I invite you at my expense, for a drink at one of my favorite places. Yes, at my expense! I get to Monaco often and would be very interested to learn if you're happy living there. Drop me a note (to Bermuda) and include your telephone number.

Anything I can do to assist in your adjustment will be "on the house". Here's hoping to see you soon!

It is likely that there will be a few additions and changes to this Report. These will be sent free if you send me a self-addressed envelope and $5 cash to cover postage and handling (I can't use stamps). Include your registration number and note if your mailing address or name is different from that of the registered buyer. As you know from previous Special Reports, I recommend that for any subscriptions, mail order items, etc. you use a "pen-name" and an address other than your home, such as a private post office box. Our records are (of course) pretty secure, and our mailing list is not for sale. But for other publishers that is not generally true. Also, incoming foreign mail in the USA can legally be opened and copied by government agencies. This is rarely done, but an ounce of caution is worth a pound of cure.

W.G. Hill, c/o S.O.S. WESTANCO, PO Box HM 1721, Hamilton, Bermuda, HMGX.

RECOMMENDED ADDITIONAL READING

Tax Havens and Their Uses. 137 pages, paperback. By Caroline Doggart. Special Report No. 186. Published and distributed by The Economist Intelligence Unit, 40 Duke Street, London W1M 5DG, United Kingdom. Price £40. One of the best comparative reports covering some two dozen locations, giving their past, present and predicted future. The book was written in 1971, and is updated every four years or so. The last edition was revised as of 1985. Excellent for an overview. *The Economist* is a respected British magazine similar to *Forbes* or *Business Week.*

International Investing by Douglas R. Casey. One of the most interesting books ever written on personal freedom, passports, extradition, and the best places in the world to live and prosper. Price about $15 from Eden Press, Box 8410, Fountain Valley, California USA 92728.

How I Found Freedom in an Unfree World by Harry Browne. Another groundbreaker, available from most bookstores, or Avon Books, 250 W. 55th St. New York City, NY 10019. How to stay out of trouble with governments, spouses, employers, litigants, and so on.

The International Harry Schultz Newsletter. Try a trial subscription at US $265. Send c/o Hill, Box 1721, Bermuda, HMGX. Ask for the "PT" reprints or the book, *PT* that I'm doing with Harry. The author is an original thinker along the same lines as your author, with emphasis on current investment recommendations (stocks, metals, real estate, etc.).

Special Report
HOW TO ESTABLISH A TAX HAVEN DOMICILE ON THE CHANNEL ISLANDS (UK) FOR £50 PER MONTH
by Dr. W.G. Hill, J.D.

A businessman, weary of government red tape, lawsuits and domestic problems, arranged to sell his business and investments for a sizeable sum. If he could keep the proceeds he would enjoy financial security with a very comfortable income. But if he had to pay all the required taxes his economic base would be cut in half.

Being both ethical and cautious, he rejected the appeals of tax shelter promoters and schemes that sounded fraudulent. "If only there was a way to keep my hard-earned money working for me instead of seeing it taken away." Then he read a government report about wealthy individuals who left their respective countries to settle in so-called tax havens. The procedure seemed so simple. He came to us and said, "This is too good to be true!" What was the government's "problem" became his solution; or was it? He asked us to determine whether establishing a tax haven domicile was (1) legal, (2) a good idea for him, and (3) how much time one actually had to spend at such a residence.

We did an in-depth investigation of the fiscal paradises of the world, and personally visited most. Our client received the original report for several thousand dollars. Since it saved him several *hundred* thousand, he was quite pleased. Our findings:

1. IS MOVING TO A TAX HAVEN LEGAL?
   Generally, yes. Almost all countries permit the free movement of their citizens. In peacetime, most nations also permit assets to be transferred abroad. But more importantly we discovered this basic principal of international law: *A government has jurisdiction (power to control) only over those people and property within its frontiers.* Once someone removes himself and the family jewels from a particular country, for all practical purposes that jurisdiction ends. (Exceptions are deportation and extradition for serious crimes.)
2. DOES IT MAKE ECONOMIC SENSE?
   For our particular client, yes indeed! We concluded that anyone who enjoyed travelling a few months a year and who was not absolutely tied down to a nine-to-five job in a high-tax country should at least consider tax havens. A mere change of legal address could typically double the income of retirees. In most cases the tax savings alone could finance all travel and living expenses. Greater financial freedom and flexibility are also factors to consider.
3. HOW MUCH TIME MUST ONE SPEND AT A TAX HAVEN?
   Domicile is normally a question of personal intention, not physical presence. Thus, a person who calls a certain place "home" can travel elsewhere for years, but his domicile will stay the same. True, some tax havens, notably Monaco, have fairly strict rules to the effect that to obtain a resident's card one must actually be physically present six months a year. But many other tax havens don't issue residence cards or even keep track of their citizens. We naturally prefer a domicile with this sort of informal approach. Residence is proven by such things as a mailing address, telephone listing, apartment lease, or house deed, etc.

HOW TO DO IT

Basically, one rents or buys suitable accommodations, arranges for appropriate identity documents, and establishes a means whereby telephone messages and mail may be held or forwarded. A checking account is opened, credit cards are obtained, and presto, the move is complete. Generally, two additional steps are also taken:

1. One or more passports are obtained from countries that do not tax non-residents. As a practical matter, this means that only USA and Philippine citizens absolutely must obtain second passports. Others may wish to do so for a variety of reasons more fully explained in our publication, THE PASSPORT REPORT.
2. All assets are expatriated from the former country. For maximum anonymity, ownership thereafter is registered in nominee banks, trusts, corporations, or agents. The funds are managed from one or more fiscal tax havens.

This Special Report gives all the details of the tax haven which proved ideal for our client. It is inexpensive: £50 per month, and this includes mail services. The initial arrangements can all be completed by mail. Assistance is given on opening a bank account and obtaining identifications, both of which require personal references at the tax haven itself. (Other people, not so well informed, have paid up to US$375,000 for arrangements that from a legal point of view, are identical.)

This particular tax haven is 100% English-speaking, and has far tougher bank-secrecy laws than Switzerland. The government is perhaps the least intrusive of any nation on earth, and is a protectorate of a major power. It is politically stable, located within commuting distance of Paris or London. It is totally free of crimes of violence or fraud. Communications are excellent.

This Special Report is available for £50, which includes surface delivery anywhere in the world. It contains all the information you will need to know about establishing your own tax haven domicile in this unique location. Payment may be by bank check, postal or other money order, Eurocheck or credit card. Amount may be £50 (Sterling) or equivalent. Add £5 or equivalent for air mail postage. Mail to: Scope Books, 62 Murray Road, Horndean, Hants. PO8 9JL, Great Britain.

REMEMBER: Personal consultations are available to all purchasers, and our money-back guarantee applies to all our publications.

THE LLOYDS REPORT
HOW TO EARN A SUBSTANTIAL OFFSHORE INCOME WITHOUT INVESTMENT
by Dr. W.G. Hill, J.D.

Some years ago a wealthy professional man was approached by a respected business associate who told him about a financial opportunity to develop a second income and asset base "offshore". I was hired as an investigator and financial consultant to report on the merit of the proposal. Since the client was promised what we regarded as a free lunch of pie in the sky, we expected to be quite negative. The deal offered was simply a partnership at Lloyds of London. All we had ever heard about Lloyds was bad news. The publicity we'd seen spoke of record losses, scandals and disputes with the British Government. On the other hand, we knew that Lloyds had been around for hundreds of years, and was the most respectable name in shipping insurance. Our client had been told that a Lloyds underwriting membership would:

1. Increase his annual income between US$50,000 and $100,000 per annum, for LIFE.
2. Open the door to excellent asset management opportunities offshore, much invaluable business information and social contacts.
3. Require no investment, only a showing of means or net worth of Sterling £100,000/US$150,000. A prior bankruptcy, criminal or fraud conviction would be a bar to membership.
4. Require neither expertise nor the investment of time or personal effort.

The partnership was relatively risk-free if a conservative agent was chosen to manage one's account, and "stop-loss" insurance was taken out.

Very sceptical of such a perfect arrangement, we accepted the challenge of doing an in-depth investigation of Lloyds as a business opportunity. The client paid $6000 for a Special Report that with his permission we have now published. Surprisingly we concluded that although a Lloyds partnership was not a one-way street to riches, it was one of the better and least risky business opportunities in the world today. We discovered a secret about all the bad publicity: It was very much like the public relations releases of a Las Vegas Casino announcing a big winner. Insurance underwriting is much like owning a gambling casino. Big losses are good business, since rates are set to cover losses and yield a profit. Without losses there would be no insurance industry. Our client eventually joined Lloyds. We have used his later experience as a case history to show all the positive and negative aspects.

The above claims were basically true! But there were some surprises, and the procedure for becoming a member was an unusual experience, to put it mildly. Our client was discouraged from joining in many conversations with people connected with Lloyds. That reason is another secret we discovered in the course of investigation. . .

Our report on this subject and all others is neither subsidized, authorized nor encouraged by the organization, countries or institutions written about. All the author has to sell is good information. Satisfaction is guaranteed. If our reports do not deliver as advertised, they may be returned (uncopied of course) for a refund.

HOW TO ORDER: All reports are £50 (Sterling) or equivalent each, post paid. Allow 6-8 weeks for surface delivery. For quicker service add £5 or equivalent for air mail. If any two reports are ordered, the third one is free. We recommend these three for the price of two, as a "package deal" because a Second Passport, a Tax Haven Refuge, and a Substantial Offshore Income and Asset Management Program is a logical combination for the person who wants to insulate himself against unexpected changes. Bank drafts, traveler's checks or currency may be sent or credit card number quoted. Checks payable to Scope Books, 62 Murray Road, Horndean, Hants. PO8 9JL, Great Britain.

PT — ALSO KNOWN AS THE FIVE FLAG THEORY: RATIONALE BEHIND THE SPECIAL REPORTS of W.G. HILL

While the titles of our other reports may not at first glimpse be of interest, if you liked THE PASSPORT REPORT we will guarantee that they will all be fascinating and useful reading for you. This series represents a coherent plan for living a stress-free, healthy and prosperous life free of governmental interference, the threat of nuclear war, taxation, and harassment. WE SOMETIMES CALL IT THE PT LIFESTYLE (PT stands for Perpetual Tourist or Prior Taxpayer).

The basic concept from Mr. Hill is that people of intelligence and wealth owe it to themselves and their descendants to have five "flags". No one with common sense should give all their assets or allegiance just to one flag. Why? Because no country nor any government has ever survived more than a few generations without totally annihilating itself or its own middle and upper classes. Even in that "last bastion of capitalism," the USA, people of property were thrice forced to flee the country. In 1780, one third (the entire middle and ruling class) was forced to move to Canada; these were the Tories who supported England in the Revolution. In 1860, it happened again; all large landowners (who supported the Confederacy in the Civil War) were forced to migrate to Mexico, Europe or South America. In the post 1917 period, prohibition, government persecutions, confiscatory inheritance taxes, compulsory military service, income taxes and suffocating government regulations once again caused most wealthy Americans and others in Europe to seek new flags. FIVE MILLION OF THE WEALTHIEST & MOST PRODUCTIVE AMERICANS LIVE ABROAD. EIGHTY-FIVE PER CENT OF ALL LIQUID PRIVATE WEALTH IS ALREADY ANONYMOUSLY REGISTERED "OFFSHORE". CAN YOU AFFORD TO HAVE ONLY ONE FLAG? — NOT IF YOUR NET WORTH IS OVER US$ 250,000.

Flag 1. BUSINESS BASE. These are the places where you make your money. Our report on Lloyds covers one attractive option. This place must be different from the place where you "legally reside" — your personal fiscal domicile. It should be at a place that gives a tax holiday to your business, freedom from over-regulation, and good access to any contacts, labor markets or materials needed for conducting the business. LONDON, TOKYO and NEW YORK are the Big Apples for Finance and Insurance. ZURICH, HONG KONG, SINGAPORE, FRANKFURT, MILAN and PANAMA are among the second rank contenders.

Flag 2. PASSPORT & CITIZENSHIP. These should be from a country which is unconcerned about its offshore citizens or what they do when outside its borders. There must be no tax or military requirement for non-residents. THE PASSPORTS MUST BE AVAILABLE TO FOREIGNERS. OUR PASSPORT REPORT IS THE FIRST BOOK TO FULLY CONSIDER THE PROPER CHOICE OF PASSPORT IN THIS CONTEXT.

Flag 3. DOMICILE. This should be a tax haven with good communication. A place where wealthy, productive people can be creative, live, relax, prosper and enjoy themselves, preferably with bank secrecy and no threat of war or revolution. Special Reports are now available on MONACO and a CHANNEL ISLAND. In process: CAMPIONE, ANDORRA, BERMUDA, THAILAND.

Flag 4. ASSET REPOSITORY. This should be a place from which assets, securities and business affairs can be managed by proxy. Requirements are the availability of highly competent financial managers, confidential banking, no tax on non-resident, non-citizens. One of the best places in which to plant your fourth flag would be Liechtenstein. Other possibilities would be AUSTRIA, LUXEMBOURG, PANAMA, NEW YORK or LONDON.

Flag 5. PLAYGROUNDS. These are the places where you would actually physically spend your time. Normally, because of legal restrictions on how long one may stay without being inducted as a taxpayer, it is necessary to have from two to four playgrounds. One might try to avoid spending more than 90 days per year in any one of them. We look for quality of life. For "no nukes" and good fishing: New Zealand. For an unbelievable sex life: Thailand, Costa Rica or the Philippines. Superb climate: California. Best food: French Riviera or Hong Kong. Stimulating cities: Paris, London, San Francisco. To buy the best things at the cheapest prices: Singapore, Hong Kong, Denmark for cars.

The W.G. Hill Special Report Series, when completed, will fully cover all Five Flags. They will be a complete guide to getting the most out of life that this Earth can offer. Each individual should have AT LEAST TWO, BUT IDEALLY THREE toeholds in each "flag". For example:

1. A BUSINESS OR SOURCE OF INCOME IN NEW YORK, LONDON AND SINGAPORE.
2. A PASSPORT FROM CANADA, BRAZIL, ITALY AND AUSTRALIA.
3. A LEGAL OR FISCAL ADDRESS IN MONACO or a CHANNEL ISLAND.
4. BANK ACCOUNTS AND OTHER ASSETS LIKE CARS OR APARTMENTS REGISTERED ANONYMOUSLY IN LIECHTENSTEIN, LONDON, LUXEMBOURG AND LUCERNE, TRUSTS OR FOUNDATIONS.
5. HANGOUTS, FRIENDS AND FUN IN PARIS, BANGKOK, MANILA, BUENOS AIRES, SYDNEY, SAN FRANCISCO.